DIGITAL DYNAMO

Mastering Networking and Public Speaking for Internet Marketers

MICHAEL LEE

ISBN: 9798860429598

Table of Contents

INTRODUCTION

Being a successful internet marketer requires more than just technical skills. It demands the ability to navigate the intricate world of networking and to deliver powerful presentations that captivate your audience.

In this dynamic era, internet marketers wield incredible influence. They have the power to transform ideas into global phenomena, businesses into industry leaders, and dreams into realities. However, behind every thriving online enterprise is an individual who not only understands the intricacies of digital marketing but also excels in the art of networking and public speaking.

Why are these skills so essential? Imagine you have a groundbreaking product or service, but no one knows about it. Or you possess the knowledge to solve a pressing problem, but your voice is lost in the digital noise. Networking and public speaking are the tools that can elevate you above the competition, opening doors to collaborations, partnerships, and a loyal customer base.

In *Digital Dynamo*, we will embark on a journey to unleash your inner strength, equipping you with the knowledge and techniques needed to excel in the realms of networking and public speaking. Whether you're a seasoned marketer looking to refine your skills or a newcomer seeking to make your mark, this guide is tailored to meet you at your current level and elevate you to new heights.

This guide isn't just about shaking hands and giving speeches; it's about becoming a force to be reckoned with in the digital arena. We'll delve into the nuances of effective online and offline networking, exploring strategies to build lasting relationships with success partners and potential customers. We'll also unravel the art of public speaking, teaching you how to craft compelling presentations that leave a lasting impact.

As we navigate through the chapters of *Digital Dynamo*, you'll discover the secrets to commanding attention, conveying your message persuasively, and inspiring action. You'll learn how to harness the power of your online presence, leverage social media platforms, and make meaningful connections in an increasingly interconnected world.

Are you ready to become a true digital dynamo? It's time to harness your inner strength and master the vital skills of networking and public speaking.

CHAPTER 1

Bridging Realms: The Synergy of Offline and Online Networking

In the ever-evolving world of internet marketing, there's a common misconception that success is solely reliant on a digital presence. However, the truth is that offline networking can be a potent catalyst for building your online empire.

Let's explore how dedicating some of your time to traditional networking methods can significantly impact your journey.

Embracing Real-World Connections

Even if your business primarily operates in the digital realm, you cannot underestimate the value of offline interactions.

These face-to-face encounters can be instrumental in fostering relationships and expanding your online reach.

Consider these avenues

Chamber of Commerce Mixers: These gatherings are hotbeds of local business activity. By attending, you can introduce yourself, articulate your online endeavors, and potentially garner valuable leads. Moreover, you might discover the ideal partner for future ventures.

Trade Shows: Trade shows offer a unique opportunity to connect with industry peers and potential clients. In this vibrant environment, you can showcase your online offerings and engage in meaningful conversations that may lead to fruitful collaborations.

Business Fairs: These events attract diverse crowds eager to explore new opportunities. Capitalize on this by presenting your online ventures and inviting attendees to join your digital journey.

Unlocking Offline Networking Tools

Beyond physical events, there are various offline networking tools at your disposal. For instance, delivering a speech about your online marketing expertise at a civic club can unlock a realm of possibilities.

This act can connect you with individuals experienced in brick-and-mortar businesses.

Mutual Learning and Collaboration: Engaging in dialogue with brick-and-mortar experts can foster mutual learning. By exchanging ideas and insights, you can potentially create hybrid solutions that benefit both parties. This collaborative spirit can spark innovation and expand your horizons.

Expanding Your Networking Horizons

Offline networking introduces an additional layer to your marketing efforts. When combined with your online strategies, it can amplify your reach exponentially. The word-of-mouth generated through your digital initiatives can be further enhanced by offline approaches.

Remember, it's all about people talking to others about who you are, what you do, and how you can help. Underestimating the power of offline networking can limit your ability to create meaningful connections, and that's a scenario you want to avoid at all costs.

A harmonious blend of online and offline networking is the key to unlocking new opportunities and expanding your online empire. Don't dismiss the real-world connections that can propel your internet marketing endeavors to greater heights.

CHAPTER 2

The Power of the 60-Second Pitch: Demystifying Internet Marketing for All

The art of the elevator speech reigns supreme. From clergy members to corporate executives, individuals from all walks of life employ this verbal tool.

An elevator speech is a concise and engaging way to convey a complete concept within the fleeting timeframe it takes an elevator to whisk you between five or six floors without pausing.

Harnessing the elevator speech technique to elucidate your vision of Internet marketing allows you to encapsulate the core essence of this complex field in just a few sentences while igniting your listener's curiosity.

Let's delve into some modernized tips on crafting your elevator speech:

A Single, Clear Definition

Kickstart your elevator speech with a clear, one-sentence definition. This initial sentence will serve as your roadmap, signposting the key aspects of Internet marketing you intend to cover.

Address Key Points Succinctly

For each point mentioned in your introductory sentence, provide a brief elaboration using one to two sentences. This focused approach ensures you stay on course, avoiding the meandering paths that can dilute your message.

Highlight Relevance

Explain the significance of each point in the context of Internet marketing, employing just a sentence or two. This brevity not only keeps you on track but also aids your listener in retaining vital information.

An effective elevator speech doesn't aim to be an exhaustive treatise on the subject. Instead, it should contain enough substance to pique your listener's interest, enticing them to explore Internet marketing further. Your compelling elevator pitch can serve as an open invitation, encouraging your audience to delve deeper into the world of Internet marketing, ideally through your marketing program.

When executed adeptly, the elevator speech can transform a mere lead into a prospective client in under a minute. That's a remarkable feat in the journey of positioning yourself for new business opportunities.

CHAPTER 3

The Name Card Revolution: Making Your Mark in the Modern World

In the digital age, where smartphones and social media dominate, the humble name card may seem like a relic of the past. However, don't be too quick to dismiss this invaluable offline marketing tool. The name card, also known as a calling card or business card, remains a powerful way to leave a lasting impression and foster meaningful connections. Here's how to make your name card stand out and serve as a gateway to future opportunities

Dare to Be Different

To make your name card truly memorable, consider stepping outside the conventional box. Start with the cardstock itself – opt for a thicker stock that not only feels substantial but also stands out from flimsy competitors. The tactile experience of holding a robust card leaves a lasting impression.

Additionally, break free from the shackles of the rectangular card. Square or round cards can be visually striking. However, ensure they still fit comfortably into standard card files; otherwise, recipients may discard them, fearing they'll be cumbersome to store.

Clarity Over Creativity

While creativity is encouraged, never sacrifice clarity for the sake of a flashy design. Using vibrant colors can help your card stand out, but prioritize legibility. Your contact information should be effortlessly readable. The goal is to facilitate easy access to your details, not to make recipients squint.

Essential Contact Information

Include crucial contact details: your name, phone number, email address, and, if possible, a fax number. While faxing may seem outdated, some individuals and businesses still rely on this communication method. Catering to various preferences ensures you're accessible to a broader audience.

An Engaging Slogan

A catchy slogan can add a touch of personality to your card. However, strike a balance – it should enhance the card's appeal without overwhelming it. Your slogan should reflect your brand's essence concisely. Remember, brevity is the soul of wit.

A Splash of Color

Don't shy away from color; it can breathe life into your name card. Just ensure it complements, rather than distracts from, your contact information. Browse online for inspiration – you might discover the perfect combination of cardstock and imagery that aligns with your image and objectives.

The name card evolves from a mere informational exchange to a statement of your personal or professional brand. Its tactile nature offers a tangible connection in an increasingly virtual world. So, don't leave home without it – your name card is your passport to building fruitful relationships and making your mark in the modern world.

CHAPTER 4

The Art of Offline Networking for Internet Marketers

In an era dominated by screens and virtual connections, the power of face-to-face networking should not be underestimated. Just as traditional businesses gather at physical events to connect and collaborate, Internet marketers can harness the benefits of offline networking. Here, we'll explore how you can strengthen your bonds with fellow Internet-based marketers in the real world.

Embrace Industry Trade Shows

Trade shows are no longer the exclusive domain of brick-and-mortar businesses. An increasing number of regional and national events cater to Internet-based enterprises and marketers. Attending these events can be incredibly beneficial.

You have two primary options when attending trade shows. You can choose to attend as a casual visitor, allowing you to explore different exhibitions and engage in conversations with fellow marketers.

Alternatively, you can become an exhibitor yourself. This not only provides opportunities to interact with fellow marketers but also puts you in the spotlight, potentially attracting new prospects.

Sponsor Local Events

Leverage your local Chamber of Commerce or civic club to host events that gather Internet marketers from your vicinity. Extend invitations to those within easy traveling distance and ensure refreshments are provided. After all, discussions tend to flow more freely over food.

This approach not only boosts your community visibility but also fosters connections with nearby marketers.

It's a win-win situation where you nurture local relationships while expanding your network.

Create a Monthly Meetup

Consider organizing a monthly caucus with Internet marketers in your community or state. If you have the space, offer to host the event; otherwise, arrange to meet at a local restaurant. These casual gatherings serve as excellent opportunities for fellowship and light business discussions.

Face-to-face encounters can lead to meaningful collaborations and lasting relationships. Sometimes, a simple meetup can spark creative ideas or reveal common challenges that prompt innovative solutions.

Leverage Online Communities for Offline Meetings

Online forums, social media groups, and professional networks are powerful tools to connect with Internet marketers. You can use these platforms to identify like-minded individuals in your area and propose offline meetups.

By combining the convenience of digital networking with the authenticity of face-to-face interactions, you can build a robust local network of Internet marketers.

These connections can lead to collaborative projects, shared insights, and even joint ventures.

While the digital landscape has transformed the business world, offline networking remains a valuable asset. Embrace the opportunity to connect with fellow Internet marketers in the real world. These in-person encounters can foster creativity, inspire innovation, and pave the way for mutually beneficial working relationships.

CHAPTER 5

Effective Follow-Up Strategies in the Digital Age

Nurturing business relationships remains as crucial as ever. Successful follow-up communication is key, even in the realm of Internet-based commerce. While the principles remain the same, modern technology has introduced new methods for building and maintaining these connections. Let's explore the art of following up using email, chat, and phone in the digital age.

The Time-Honored Telephone Call

The telephone call has been a cornerstone of business follow-up for decades. It's an opportunity to ensure customer satisfaction, identify additional needs, and solidify the relationship between vendor and client. For Internet-based businesses, this method is equally relevant.

A post-purchase phone call serves multiple purposes:

Customer Satisfaction: It's a chance to ensure that customers are content with their purchase.

Identifying Needs: Businesses can uncover other needs that their products or services can address.

Building Rapport: Personal connections are strengthened, increasing the likelihood of repeat business.

The Versatility of Email

Email has emerged as a versatile follow-up tool. Many customers prefer this approach, as it grants them the flexibility to respond at their convenience. Unlike phone calls, email allows clients to take their time crafting responses without feeling rushed.

Key Advantages of email follow-up include

Convenient Timing: Clients can respond when it suits them, promoting a relaxed and thoughtful exchange.

Accessibility: Email is universally accessible and can be used for various purposes, from thanking clients for their business to sharing updates and resources.

Embracing Real-Time Chat

Real-time chat has surged in popularity as businesses increasingly rely on digital tools. If a client has provided a screen name for chat, it's an open invitation for follow-up communication. Even when clients are offline, many systems allow sending offline messages that they can access upon logging in.

The benefits of real-time chat follow-ups

Instant Communication: Clients appreciate the immediacy of chat, making it ideal for quick inquiries or assistance.

Ease of Use: With the prevalence of chat interfaces, clients are comfortable with this mode of communication.

Balance and Frequency

A golden rule for all forms of follow-up is to strike the right balance and respect clients' preferences. Not all clients welcome frequent contact. Some may appreciate weekly interactions, while others find anything more than monthly follow-ups intrusive.

Understanding your clients' preferences and respecting their comfort zones is essential. It fosters healthier working relationships and ensures that your follow-up efforts are received positively.

Follow-up communication remains a vital component of building and sustaining business relationships. In the digital age, the tools have evolved, but the core principles of nurturing connections, identifying needs, and providing excellent service remain unchanged.

Mastering the art of follow-up in today's technology-driven landscape can significantly enhance your business's success.

CHAPTER 6

The Power of Charisma in Seminar Coaching

Whether you're conducting workshops online or in person, charisma plays a pivotal role in engaging your audience and leaving a lasting impact. Beyond the mere transmission of information, your ability to captivate, connect, and inspire your audience is what sets you apart. Charisma isn't about being someone you're not; it's about enhancing your natural attributes to create a dynamic coaching persona that resonates with your audience.

Understanding Charisma

Charisma can manifest differently from one person to another, but the outcome is universal: you want people to not only listen to you but to trust, respect, and genuinely like you. Cultivating your coaching persona involves focusing on qualities that come naturally to you.

Authenticity is key; trying to emulate someone else can come off as artificial and unconvincing.

Attributes of a Charismatic Seminar Coach

Humor: Humor is a universal icebreaker. It helps people relax and creates an enjoyable atmosphere. Injecting humor into your coaching sessions doesn't mean you need to become a stand-up comedian. Instead, use it strategically to set a comfortable tone for learning and engagement.

Accessible Language: While some technical terms may be necessary, keeping your language accessible is crucial. Think of your seminar as a friendly conversation, not a lecture. Simplify complex ideas and present them in a way that anyone can understand. This approach eases comprehension and encourages participation.

Engage with the Audience: Interactivity is key. Provide opportunities for your audience to ask questions or share their thoughts. This can be done verbally or through written means for those who prefer privacy. Encouraging participation fosters a sense of involvement and inclusivity.

Transitioning to Web Conferencing

If you're accustomed to in-person coaching but are venturing into web conferencing, rest assured that your charisma can shine through the digital medium as well. Authenticity should remain consistent whether you're in front of a live audience or a virtual one. This continuity reinforces your credibility and authenticity, making you relatable across different settings.

Charisma is the secret ingredient that elevates your seminar coaching. It's not about being someone else; it's about being the best version of yourself. Humor, accessible language, and audience engagement are your tools for success, regardless of whether you're coaching in person or through web conferencing. Charisma is a powerful force that bridges the gap between knowledge sharing and inspiring transformation.

CHAPTER 7

Mastering Stage Confidence

Stage fright is an experience that transcends careers, affecting actors, politicians, and public figures alike. It's essential to understand that stage fright is a natural human response to a social situation, and it's far from uncommon. While some people feel their anxiety subside once they're on stage, others may struggle with lingering unease. Here, we'll explore strategies to overcome stage fright and perform with confidence.

Understanding Stage Fright

Before delving into strategies, it's crucial to demystify stage fright. First, realize that stage fright won't harm you; it's your body's way of preparing for a challenge. The initial anxiety you feel is the result of a surge of adrenaline, which your body naturally regulates. In essence, it's a brief bout of heightened alertness.

The Fear of Embarrassment

Many individuals experience stage fright due to the fear of embarrassment. To overcome this fear, remind yourself of your preparation and professionalism. You are well-prepared and capable, and the audience is there to learn from you. Trust in your competence; this will help dispel the anxiety stemming from the fear of making a fool of yourself.

Connect with Your Audience

Instead of seeing a sea of faces, identify a few friendly and welcoming individuals in the audience. Speak to them as if you're having a one-on-one conversation. This technique shifts your focus away from the crowd and helps alleviate anxiety. As you become more comfortable, expand your conversational reach to include more audience members.

Embrace Stage Fright

Stage fright isn't the enemy; it's a useful tool that keeps you mentally sharp. It's similar to how stage actors feel uneasy if they don't experience stage fright before a performance because it helps maintain alertness. Embrace stage fright as your mind's way of gearing you up for a stellar presentation.

Practical Techniques for Confidence

In addition to mental strategies, consider practical techniques to boost your confidence:

Visualization: Before taking the stage, visualize yourself confidently delivering your presentation. This mental rehearsal can significantly reduce anxiety.

Practice: Thoroughly rehearse your presentation. Familiarity with your content boosts confidence. Consider practicing in front of a trusted friend or colleague to simulate the presentation environment.

Breathing Exercises: Deep breathing exercises can help calm your nerves. Practice slow, deep breaths to reduce anxiety before and during your presentation.

Physical Activity: Engaging in light physical activity, like stretching or a brief walk, before your presentation can reduce tension and anxiety.

Stage fright is a common human response that can be managed and even harnessed to enhance your performance. Understand that it won't harm you, focus on your preparation and professionalism, connect with your audience, and embrace the initial anxiety as a tool for peak performance.

With practice and these techniques, you can overcome stage fright and confidently shine on any stage.

CHAPTER 8

Mastering Live Internet Marketing Presentations

Live presentations on internet marketing may seem like a different beast altogether, but the truth is, they share foundational principles with online presentations. To give a compelling live presentation, you don't need to reinvent the wheel; instead, enhance the basics with your online expertise. Here are some strategies to make your live internet marketing presentation as engaging as your online work.

Visual Aids: Elevate Engagement

Online presentations often rely on visual elements like slides, images, and animations. What many forget is that these tools have been used effectively offline for ages. Utilize a large screen to project your slides, images, and animations as a backdrop for your speech. This combination of visual and auditory stimulation will connect with a broad audience.

Be Animated: Convey Enthusiasm

While you don't need to be in constant motion, let your facial expressions and tone of voice convey your enthusiasm for the subject. A dynamic and engaging presenter tends to captivate the audience. Authenticity in your presentation style goes a long way in keeping the audience engaged.

Strategic Breaks: Foster Understanding

Ensure your presentation allows the audience to absorb the information. A helpful guideline is not to present more than twenty minutes of information at a stretch. After this interval, introduce a change, such as a question-and-answer session, a short break, or group activities for brainstorming. These variations keep the presentation fresh and dynamic.

Casual Atmosphere: Encourage Engagement

Relaxed audiences are more attentive. Encourage a casual mood during your presentation. Engage with your audience on a personal level, fostering a sense of connection. When people feel comfortable, they tend to listen more intently. If they get engrossed in your presentation, the time will seem to fly by.

Master Positive Body Language

Effective body language can make a world of difference. Maintain eye contact with the audience, use open and inviting postures, and smile genuinely. These non-verbal cues communicate your confidence and eagerness, creating a more engaging atmosphere.

Varied Delivery: Keep It Fresh

Variety is key to keeping your audience's attention. Introduce different elements into your presentation, such as anecdotes, case studies, or live demonstrations. These changes in format help break the monotony and maintain audience interest.

Interactive Elements: Engage Your Audience

Engage your audience actively. Encourage questions and participation throughout the presentation. Interactive elements like polls or live chats can make the audience feel involved and invested in the content.

When you master the art of live internet marketing presentations, you can connect with your audience on a deeper level.

By incorporating visual aids, maintaining enthusiasm, offering strategic breaks, fostering a casual atmosphere, mastering body language, introducing variety, and engaging your audience, you'll not only capture their attention but also leave a lasting impression. Remember, effective presentations are rooted in human connection, whether online or offline.

CHAPTER 9

Mastering the Art of Quick Sales in Internet Marketing

In the world of Internet marketing, the first five minutes can make or break a sale. Customers often decide whether or not they're interested in a product within this brief window of opportunity. As a successful Internet marketer, your challenge is to maximize these crucial five minutes.

Several pivotal elements unfold within this timespan

Attraction and Engagement: During the initial five minutes, a customer decides if the product is worth further exploration. If it doesn't capture their interest, even the most persuasive pitch won't change their mind.

Identifying Obstacles: Customers also use this time to identify potential obstacles that might deter them from making a purchase. If they perceive any significant barriers, it can render everything following those initial minutes ineffective.

Your goal is to not only grab the customer's attention but also to help them envision how the product can significantly benefit them.

Here's a strategic approach to make the most of these crucial moments:

Understand Customer Needs: Begin by thoroughly understanding your customer's needs. Ask probing questions that help you tailor your presentation to their specific requirements. For instance, if a customer's primary concern is paying their phone bill, demonstrate how your product directly addresses this need.

Proactively Address Common Objections: Anticipate and address common objections customers might raise. Many of these objections are universal, shared by people from various backgrounds. By bringing up and swiftly dispelling these concerns in the first five minutes, you can keep the customer engaged and interested.

Emphasize Benefits: Always close your pitch by emphasizing the benefits of your product. These benefits should extend beyond overcoming obstacles. Continuing with the phone bill example, illustrate how your product can make paying the bill easier every month, not just for the current month.

By perfecting your approach within these initial five minutes, you significantly increase your chances of closing the sale. Invest time in crafting and refining your presentation model, seeking feedback, and honing your skills.

This preparation will empower you to navigate real sales situations with confidence and skill. Remember, in Internet marketing, these crucial five minutes are your prime opportunity to capture your audience and drive sales.

CHAPTER 10

Leveraging Social Media for Networking and Public Speaking

Social media platforms have evolved into essential tools for Internet marketers looking to expand their network and excel in public speaking engagements. This chapter delves into the art of leveraging social media for networking and mastering the public speaking arena.

The Social Media Revolution

Social media platforms have transformed how we communicate, share information, and build connections. These platforms are no longer just for keeping in touch with friends and family; they're also powerful networking and marketing tools.

Whether you're a seasoned marketer or just starting, embracing social media is key to staying relevant in the digital age.

Creating Your Professional Persona

Before you begin using social media for networking and public speaking, it's vital to curate your online persona. Start by updating your profiles to reflect your expertise, skills, and professional experiences.

Use a high-quality profile picture and write a compelling bio that highlights your strengths as an Internet marketer and public speaker. Remember, your social media profiles often serve as your digital business card.

Choosing the Right Platforms

Not all social media platforms are created equal. Each has its unique audience and purpose. To leverage social media effectively, you must choose the right platforms for your goals. Here are some popular platforms and their primary uses:

LinkedIn: Often referred to as the professional network, LinkedIn is ideal for B2B networking. Share your achievements, connect with industry peers, and join relevant groups to expand your network.

Twitter: A fast-paced platform, Twitter is great for sharing quick updates, industry news, and engaging in real-time conversations with your audience. Use relevant hashtags to increase your visibility.

Instagram: Visual content rules on Instagram. Showcase your public speaking engagements, share behind-the-scenes glimpses of your work, and use Instagram Stories to interact with your followers.

Facebook: While it's a versatile platform, Facebook is excellent for building communities and hosting live events. Create a professional page to share your expertise and engage with your audience through posts, live sessions, and groups.

YouTube: If you're comfortable in front of the camera, YouTube is a powerful platform for sharing your public speaking sessions, tutorials, and interviews. Create a dedicated channel to showcase your expertise.

Engagement Strategies

Once you've established your online presence, focus on building meaningful relationships with your audience.

Engagement is key to successful networking and public speaking:

Consistent Content: Regularly share valuable content related to your niche. This can include blog posts, infographics, videos, and more. Consistency keeps your audience engaged.

Interact Authentically: Respond to comments and messages in a genuine and timely manner. Engaging with your audience fosters trust and credibility.

Networking Groups: Join relevant networking groups or communities on platforms like LinkedIn and Facebook. These groups are ideal for connecting with like-minded professionals and sharing your expertise.

Live Sessions: Host live sessions where you discuss industry trends, offer tips, or conduct Q&A sessions. Live videos often receive more interaction than pre-recorded content.

Collaborations: Partner with other influencers or experts in your niche for co-hosted webinars or social media takeovers. This cross-promotion can significantly expand your reach.

Mastering Public Speaking via Social Media

Social media can also serve as a training ground for your public speaking skills:

Practice Makes Perfect: Start by sharing short video snippets discussing industry topics. Gradually increase the length and complexity of your videos as you become more comfortable.

Feedback Loop: Encourage your audience to provide feedback and ask questions. Use their input to refine your content and presentation style.

Webinars and Live Workshops: As your confidence grows, consider hosting webinars or live workshops through platforms like Zoom or Facebook Live. Promote these events on your social media channels.

Audience Engagement: During your public speaking sessions, encourage audience participation by asking questions or conducting polls. This interaction keeps your audience engaged.

Consistent Branding: Maintain a consistent brand image across all your social media profiles and public speaking engagements. This creates a cohesive and memorable online presence.

Social media offers a wealth of opportunities for Internet marketers looking to expand their network and enhance their public speaking skills. By curating your professional persona, selecting the right platforms, and engaging authentically, you can leverage social media to reach a broader audience and become a confident public speaker in the digital age.

CHAPTER 11

The Art of Online Webinars and Workshops

In the ever-evolving landscape of digital marketing and professional development, online webinars and workshops have become indispensable tools. This chapter explores the art of creating and conducting impactful webinars and workshops that engage your audience, establish your authority, and drive your Internet marketing success to new heights.

The Power of Online Learning

Online learning has experienced a significant boom in recent years, and for a good reason. It provides accessibility, flexibility, and the ability to connect with a global audience.

As an Internet marketer, harnessing the potential of online webinars and workshops can set you apart as an expert in your field.

Defining Webinars and Workshop

Before delving into the intricacies, let's distinguish between webinars and workshops:

Webinars: These are online seminars that allow you to present information, interact with your audience, and answer questions in real-time. Webinars can be one-way presentations or interactive sessions, depending on your goals.

Workshops: Workshops are hands-on, interactive sessions where participants actively engage with the content. They often involve exercises, group discussions, and practical applications of the material.

Creating Impactful Webinars

Define Your Goals: Start by outlining your objectives. Are you aiming to educate, promote a product, or build your brand's authority? Knowing your goals will shape your webinar's content and structure.

Engaging Content: Craft a compelling narrative that captures your audience's attention from the start. Use multimedia elements like slides, videos, and infographics to enhance your presentation.

Interactivity: Encourage audience participation through polls, Q&A sessions, and chat discussions. Engaged participants are more likely to remember and act on your message.

Timing: Be mindful of your webinar's length. Most successful webinars last between 30 minutes to an hour. Ensure you allocate time for your main presentation and audience interactions.

Promotion: Market your webinar effectively through email lists, social media, and your website. Create a sense of urgency to encourage registrations.

Test Run: Conduct a practice run to ensure your technology works smoothly. Familiarize yourself with the webinar platform's features, and have a backup plan in case of technical issues.

Post-Webinar Follow-Up: Send a thank-you email to attendees, share the recording for those who missed it, and gather feedback to improve future webinars.

Designing Impactful Workshops

Clear Objectives: Define the workshop's learning objectives. What should participants take away? Structure your content around achieving these goals.

Interactive Activities: Plan engaging activities that encourage active participation. Group discussions, case studies, and hands-on exercises make workshops memorable.

Materials: Provide participants with resources, handouts, or workbooks to support their learning during and after the workshop.

Facilitation Skills: As the workshop leader, your facilitation skills are crucial.

Foster a supportive and inclusive environment, and encourage open dialogue among participants.

Feedback: Collect feedback throughout and after the workshop to gauge its effectiveness and identify areas for improvement.

Combining Webinars and Workshops

Consider blending webinars and workshops to create comprehensive learning experiences. For example, start with a webinar to introduce a topic and generate interest, then follow up with a workshop to delve deeper and allow participants to apply what they've learned.

Monetizing Webinars and Workshops

If your webinars and workshops offer substantial value, you can monetize them through ticket sales or subscription models. Ensure that your content justifies the cost and provides tangible benefits to participants.

Online webinars and workshops are potent tools in your Internet marketing arsenal. When thoughtfully designed and expertly delivered, they can establish your authority, engage your audience, and drive your success to new heights. Mastering the art of webinars and workshops is an investment that pays dividends in your professional journey.

CHAPTER 12

Navigating Challenges and Ethical Considerations

In your journey as a digital dynamo, mastering networking and public speaking for Internet marketing, it's essential to navigate the challenges and ethical considerations that arise in this dynamic landscape. This chapter explores the common obstacles you might face and how to maintain ethical integrity in your endeavors.

The Challenges You May Encounter

Technical Glitches: The digital realm isn't immune to technical issues. Whether it's a webinar platform malfunction or a disrupted internet connection during a live presentation, these hiccups can be stressful. Prepare by having backup plans and remaining calm under pressure.

Audience Engagement: Keeping your online audience engaged can be challenging. Distractions are just a click away, and it's easy for participants to lose focus.

Implement interactive elements, ask questions, and encourage participation to combat this challenge.

Content Saturation: The internet is flooded with content. Standing out amid the noise can be difficult.

To overcome this, focus on creating high-quality, unique content that addresses your audience's specific needs.

Time Management: Balancing the demands of Internet marketing, networking, and public speaking can be overwhelming.

Effective time management and prioritization are essential skills to develop.

Feedback and Criticism: Not everyone will be receptive to your message, and you may encounter criticism.

Embrace constructive feedback as an opportunity for growth and ignore unwarranted negativity.

Maintaining Ethical Integrity

As an Internet marketer, your reputation and long-term success rely on ethical practices. Here are some key considerations:

Transparency: Be transparent about your intentions, products, and affiliations. Avoid misleading claims or false advertising.

Privacy: Respect user privacy by adhering to data protection laws and obtaining consent for data collection. Protect customer information from breaches.

Honesty: Be honest about your products or services. Avoid deceptive practices such as fake testimonials or reviews.

Respect: Treat your audience, peers, and competitors with respect. Engage in healthy competition and avoid unethical tactics to gain an advantage.

Compliance: Stay informed about relevant laws and regulations in your industry, such as GDPR or FTC guidelines. Ensure your practices align with legal requirements.

Authenticity: Be authentic in your online persona. Authenticity builds trust and fosters genuine connections with your audience.

Accountability: Take responsibility for your actions and rectify any mistakes promptly. Accountability demonstrates integrity.

Dealing with Ethical Dilemmas

In the fast-paced world of Internet marketing, you might encounter ethical dilemmas. Here's how to address them:

Consult Ethics Guidelines: Refer to industry-specific ethical guidelines, such as those provided by marketing associations, for guidance.

Seek Advice: Discuss the dilemma with mentors or trusted colleagues to gain different perspectives.

Pause and Reflect: Take time to reflect on the situation, considering the potential consequences of each action.

Choose Integrity: In challenging situations, prioritize ethical considerations over short-term gains.

Learn and Improve: Use ethical dilemmas as opportunities for personal and professional growth. Learn from your experiences to avoid similar situations in the future.

Navigating the challenges and ethical considerations of Internet marketing, networking, and public speaking is an ongoing process.

By proactively addressing challenges and upholding ethical standards, you'll not only build a strong reputation but also contribute positively to the digital marketing community.

Embrace these principles as you continue your journey as a digital dynamo, mastering the art of networking and public speaking for Internet marketing.

Conclusion

Unleashing Opportunities in the Offline World

As you wrap up this journey into the realms of digital dynamism, it's important to remember that while your primary focus may be the online world, the offline realm offers its own set of dynamic opportunities. In fact, the synergy between online and offline interactions has ushered in a new era of possibilities, and your task is to recognize and harness these opportunities to your advantage.

Here's how to uncover more avenues for success in the offline world:

Network with Multiverse Marketers: Extend your horizons by connecting with marketers who navigate both the digital and physical domains. Engaging with these multifaceted individuals can open doors to innovative offline marketing techniques that complement your online efforts.

Seek Wisdom from Your Audience: Your loyal customers are a goldmine of insights. Solicit feedback from them on what they'd like to see from your business in the offline realm. Their suggestions may provide the seeds for unique offline initiatives that seamlessly align with your current business model.

Think Like a Consumer: Take off your entrepreneur hat and step into the shoes of a consumer. What drives your offline purchases? Can you integrate any of these motivations into your existing business to expand your offline presence effectively?

Study the Competition: Keep an eagle eye on your competitors. Analyze their strategies for expanding into the offline world. Some of their approaches might be just the inspiration you need to broaden your horizons offline.

Opportunities don't always arrive neatly wrapped, ready to be unwrapped like a child's toy. More often, it requires a keen eye to spot the potential, relate it to your current circumstances, and figure out how to integrate the concept into your business model. Embrace your creativity and explore the multifaceted tools available in both online and offline environments.

In this ever-evolving landscape of digital dynamism, your adaptability and innovative thinking are your greatest assets.

Keep your senses attuned to the possibilities that emerge as the online and offline worlds continue to intersect. By leveraging the opportunities that span these diverse landscapes, you're well-equipped to achieve new heights of success and make your mark as a true digital dynamo.

Your journey doesn't end here; it merely enters a new phase, rich with uncharted territory and boundless opportunities. Stay dynamic, stay creative, and continue to unleash your inner strength as you forge ahead in the world of Internet marketing, networking, and public speaking. Your future is yours to shape, both online and offline.

9 798860 429598